MARK BRUNELL

Super Southpaw

by

Pete Prisco

SPORTS PUBLISHING INC.
www.SportsPublishingInc.com

Production manager: Susan M. McKinney
Production coordinator: Erin J. Sands
Series editor: Rob Rains
Cover design: Scot Muncaster/Todd Lauer
Photo coordinator: Claudia Mitroi
Photos: AP/Wide World Photos, Joe Robbins, Brian Spurlock

ISBN: 1-58261-166-1
Library of Congress Catalog Card Number: 99-68299

SPORTS PUBLISHING INC.
SportsPublishingInc.com

Printed in the United States.

Contents

Mark using some fancy footwork to run for a touchdown.
(Joe Robbins)

CHAPTER ONE

Arrival Time

The clock showed just over three minutes left in the game, and the Jacksonville Jaguars led the Denver Broncos 23-20 in the 1996 AFC Divisional playoffs. That in itself was news enough, as the Jaguars had come into the game as 15-point underdogs, meaning few gave them a chance.

Yet here they were just three minutes away from a Joe Namath-like upset, thanks in large part to the play of their quarterback, Mark Brunell.

Mark warms up before a game.
(AP/World Wide Photos)

On the same field made famous by Denver's John Elway, Mark was in the process of stealing the show from the future Hall of Famer. Using both his legs - scrambling for big gains time and again - and his arm, Mark had this second-year expansion team on the verge of moving one game away from the Super Bowl.

Three minutes was all that stood in the Jaguars way. Not to mention Elway, the king of the comeback. With Elway on the other sideline, Mark knew he needed more points, and more than just a field goal.

Faced with a third-and-5 at the Denver 16, Mark called time out to talk to his teammates and the coaching staff. On the sideline, he spoke with receiver Jimmy Smith.

"If they play you in press (tight man)," Mark said, "run a fade."

Mark carries the ball himself to help set up a touchdown. (Joe Robbins)

At the line, the Broncos were indeed in a press. Mark didn't have to say a thing as the ball was snapped. Smith ran the fade. Mark threw a perfect pass that came down into Smith's diving hands for a touchdown.

Jacksonville 30, Denver 20.

"All I had to do was hold my hands out," said Smith. "The pass was perfect."

The 10-point lead proved even too much for Elway and his comeback magic. The Jaguars won 30-27 in what was the biggest playoff upset in years.

It would prove to be the coming-out party for Mark. He completed 18 of 29 passes for 245 yards and two touchdowns. He also ran for 44 yards on seven carries, including an amazing 29-yard run to help set up the final touchdown. He led the Jaguars to scores on their final six possessions of the game against a team that came into the game with the best record in the AFC.

"Mark Brunell is going to be a household name," Smith said after that game.

The lefthander who had patiently waited his time, first in college at the University of Washington and then again in the NFL playing behind Brett Favre in Green Bay, did become a household name that day. It's the day Mark arrived as an NFL quarterback, the day the Jaguars officially became his team.

It was also a day for a nation to take note as this Steve Young-clone, wearing the same No. 8 jersey, outperformed John Elway in his own backyard.

The Jaguars' dream season did end the next week in Foxboro, Mass., when they lost 20-6 to the New England Patriots, stopping them one game short of the Super Bowl. Shortly after that game, Mark stopped to reflect on the season, one that had kids in Jacksonville scurrying to buy his No. 8 jersey.

"It was special," Mark said. "And it's something for us to build on. It's something for me to build on. This is only the beginning."

Was he ever right.

At one point in his career, Mark had to decide between baseball and football. (Joe Robbins)

2

Baseball or Football?

Baseball was Mark's first love as kid, aside from wearing his favorite cowboy uniform, and, no, that wasn't a Roger Staubach jersey.

"I wouldn't go anywhere unless I had the hat and the boots and the six-shooter on my side," Mark said.

He soon outgrew that, with sports his new passion. Growing up in Santa Maria, California, a farming community 11 miles from the Pacific Ocean, it was hard for Mark not to like baseball. His dad was the varsity coach at the high school for one, and he was very good at it for another. Playing since he was five, baseball came naturally to him.

With his strong left arm, Mark excelled as a pitcher. He eventually earned all-conference honors in high school all four years, and was drafted in 1992 by the Atlanta Braves.

But by then, football had his heart.

"Football was more exciting," Mark said. "I had played so much baseball at that point. I wasn't burned out. But the game was just slow. The practices were long and slow. With football, it's boom, boom for two hours.

"But I think I was better in baseball than I was in football. Baseball came much easier to me. Football was more of a challenge."

Those who watched him play baseball still get excited about his abilities—and what might have been.

"No doubt in my mind Mark would be playing major-league baseball right now if he didn't pursue football," said Mike Denne, who coached Mark's football team in high school. "He could hit with power, throw, field, run. What more do you want?"

Mark wanted excitement, which football gave him. At the age of 10, he moved from fullback to quarterback, which seemed natural with his strong left arm, the same arm that he once used to playfully shoot the six-shooter.

Now he was a gunslinger of a different kind.

It wasn't until after his freshman year at St. Joseph's High School that Mark knew football would be his main sport. He attended a camp that summer at UCLA that convinced him throwing spirals beat throwing curve balls any day.

"Baseball became just something to do rather

than his real passion," said his father, Dave, who along with wife, Sharon, raised Mark and his younger brother, Matt. "Baseball was no longer his first love. He was no longer interested in hitting extra or working on his pitching once he decided to play football."

During his three years as the starter at St. Joseph, Mark led the Knights to a 20-7 record, earning all-conference honors. He's the only player in Santa Barbara County to earn player of the year honors in two different sports. Yes, football and baseball - a feat unmatched by area players Randall Cunningham and Robin Ventura.

As a quarterback, Mark threw for 5,893 yards and 41 touchdowns, while also playing safety. All the while, he maintained a 3.92 grade point average and stayed away from trouble, earning the respect of his coaches and recruitment by major schools to play football and baseball.

"My dad was my role model," said Mark. "When he said, 'make sure you get your homework done before you do anything else,' I did it. When my mom said, 'wash the dishes or go make up your room,' I just did it. It was the thing to do. I respected them. That's just the way you're supposed to do things."

The only trouble Mark would get into was fighting with his younger brother. Four years younger than Mark, Matt would always be available for wresting matches on the family-room floor. In fact, it's something the two still do, even clearing out a hotel room the night before a road game against Oakland in 1996.

"They're wrestling full bore," said Mark's father, Dave, remembering the night in Oakland. "Their shirts were torn. It's not like they were fight-

Mark was the only player in Santa Barbara County to earn player of the year honors in baseball and football. (Joe Robbins)

ing. Just a couple of brothers having fun."

That fun helped seed the competitive desire that still drives Mark today. Whether it's beating up on little brother or beating the Broncos, Mark is all business.

"He hates to lose," said Jaguars tackle Tony Boselli, who is Mark's best friend. "He's as competitive as anyone I know. At anything. He may be calm off the field, but when he's competing, he's as hard-nosed as anyone I know."

"When I get on the field I get so competitive," said Mark. "Winning is so important to me."

That drive helped earn Mark a scholarship to play football at Washington, although he could have played both sports at UCLA and Stanford. Football had replaced baseball as his sport of choice.

It would prove, years later, to be the right choice.

Mark dodges past a fallen opponent. (Joe Robbins)

CHAPTER THREE

Football it is!

The gridiron wasn't kind to Mark his first two years at Washington. Playing for legendary coach Don James, Mark redshirted his first season in 1988, then was a little-used backup in 1989 behind Cary Conklin. He threw just 12 passes that season.

Had he made the right decision to play football?

In 1990, that answer became a resounding yes.

Mark earned the starting job, playing every game for the Huskies as the team won the Pac-10 title—their first since 1981—and a trip to the Rose Bowl. Mark's passing, which accounted for 1,732 yards and two touchdowns on the season, was a big reason the Huskies got to the 1991 Rose Bowl.

His legs were another reason. Mark showed the first signs of the athletic ability he would carry to the NFL as he rushed for 444 yards and scored 10 touchdowns.

His arm and his legs led Washington to the Rose Bowl victory over Iowa. That day, Mark completed 14 of 22 passes for 163 yards and two touchdowns. He also ran for two touchdowns, earning MVP honors in the process.

Right decision to play football? You bet.

The high time, though, soon turned to a low, the lowest of Mark's athletic career. Poised for a big season in 1991, Mark was getting recognition from around the country. The Huskies were too, being tabbed as an early preseason top 10 team in the spring of 1991, with Mark a big reason why.

Then disaster hit. During a mostly meaningless spring practice, Mark tore the anterior cruciate ligament in his left knee. It was an injury that doctors feared would put him on the sidelines for the 1991 season.

Mark knew otherwise. The competitive drive, the desire to be the best, fueled his recovery. Nothing, not a devastating knee injury, was going to ruin his entire season.

He told Washington coach Don James just that before surgery on the knee.

"The last thing he said before surgery was 'Stanford,'" James said.

Stanford was Washington's opponent in the 1991 opener. Mark was recovering mentally, even before the surgery.

"I knew in my mind that I could, with hard work, make it back," Mark said. "I didn't want to miss the whole season."

He didn't. While he didn't make it back for the Stanford game—a real longshot at best—Mark did return for the final four games of the season, sharing time with Billy Joe Hobert. The Huskies finished 12-0 that year, and were co-national champions with the University of Miami.

Mark helped Washington win its second consecutive Rose Bowl, beating Michigan 34-14. Sharing time with Hobert, Mark completed seven of eight passes for 89 yards and one touchdown in that game. After the season, he was named the team's most-inspirational player.

"You couldn't have criticized anyone for not coming back," said James. "But he made up his mind he wasn't going to miss the season."

Determination. Drive. Will to succeed.

Mark was displaying it all again.

Then baseball re-entered his life. In the summer of 1992, as he prepared for his senior season, the Atlanta Braves drafted him and offered him a $7,500 contract to play for their A-league team. The amazing thing about that is Mark hadn't played baseball since high school.

Mark seriously toyed with the idea of signing with the Braves. The knee injury had somewhat clouded his football career, and he was a young newlywed with a baby daughter. Playing baseball would be a whole lot easier than the construction jobs he worked in the summer to make ends meet.

"I gave it some thought," Mark said. "For us, back then, that was a big chunk of money."

Before making his decision, Mark leaned on the one person who constantly gave him advice his entire life, sometimes advice he would tune out as the two drove to school during his high school years. This time, he didn't tune his father out.

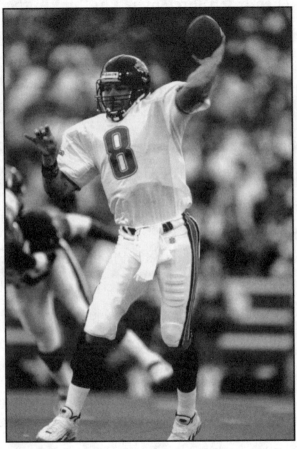

As a result of his decision to stick with football, Mark ended up playing for the Jacksonville Jaguars. (Joe Robbins)

This time, Dave Brunell told his son to stick with football.

"He said, 'everything is OK, Mark, just stick with football,'" Mark recalled. "I didn't know what was going to happen."

The next year Mark again was forced to share time with Hobert, starting the last half of the season and earning second-team All-Pac-10 honors. The Huskies again went to the Rose Bowl, but this time they lost to Michigan, but not because of Mark. He completed 18 of 30 passes for 308 yards and two touchdowns. Mark finished his career completing 259 of 498 passes for 3,423 yards, 23 touchdowns and 16 interceptions.

The following spring, when it came time for the NFL draft, Mark knew for sure he had made the right decision in sticking with football.

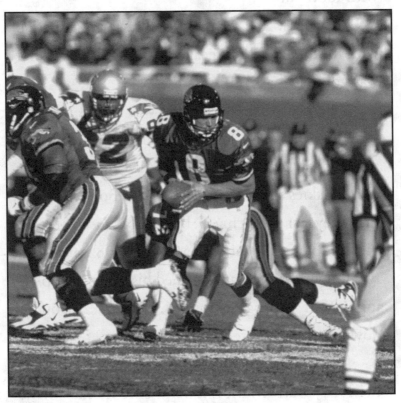

Mark rolls left against the Patriots. (Joe Robbins)

CHAPTER FOUR

Draft Day

Draft day can be a tough time for college prospects. You sit and wait and hope that somebody will call your name.

Please, let it be me.

Mark knows all about that.

Upon the conclusion of his college career, Mark was viewed as an athletic quarterback with a good arm, but one with injury concerns. The knee injury would not go away.

It hung above him like a black cloud. It went

In 1996, Mark had the fifth-most prolific single-season performance by a quarterback in NFL history. (Joe Robbins)

with him to Indianapolis for the NFL combine in February of 1993 as doctors from all 28 teams poked and prodded him to see if he had truly recovered from that devastating injury.

Could one of the most mobile quarterbacks in the country maintain that style in the NFL?

The top quarterbacks entering the draft that year were Drew Bledsoe of Washington State - Mark's rival - and Rick Mirer of Notre Dame. Mark was ranked further down the line, behind even Hobert.

Bledsoe went first that year to the New England Patriots, where he has become a star. Mirer went second to the Seattle Seahawks, where he flopped. Hobert went in the third round to the Los Angeles Raiders.

Mark had to wait.

With family and friends gathered as his house in Santa Maria, the call didn't come until the fifth round when the Green Bay Packers drafted him. The Packers worked him out that spring, and coach Mike Holmgren came away impressed.

One problem. The Packers already had a quarterback - a guy named Brett Favre.

If they hadn't, Holmgren later said he would have used a second-round pick on Mark, that's how highly he thought of him, despite the knee injury. In the fifth round, the Packers felt they got a steal.

"I remember being so happy to get drafted after waiting so long," said Mark.

That excitement was tempered a bit when the reality of the situation became obvious. Favre was entrenched as the starter; Mark would have to wait his turn.

As it turned out, he did a lot of waiting in Green Bay. He never started a game for the Packers, passing for just 95 yards in two seasons. Yet Mark says his time in Green Bay was invaluable.

"I wanted to play," Mark said, "but it was a balance between wanting to play and knowing I needed to learn. A lot of young quarterbacks get thrown into a situation where they have to play right now. That's the best way to learn - the on-the-field experience - but they go through a hard time. I was fortunate. I got very good teaching in Green Bay. And I got to sit and watch Brett. He struggled those first couple of years, so I got to see him grow."

The learning process was helped by then-Green Bay quarterbacks coach Steve Mariucci, who is now the head coach of the San Francisco 49ers. Mariucci had a close relationship with his quarterbacks, a relationship that still exists.

"Steve helped all of us," said Mark. "It was a great learning experience playing under him and Mike."

The only real playing Mark did came in the

No one is more focused than Mark. (Joe Robbins)

preseason. It was during the 1994 preseason that one coach in particular became intrigued by this scrambling, younger version of Steve Young.

That coach was Tom Coughlin, whose task was the build the Jaguars from scratch.

Coughlin had been hired in 1994, a year prior to the Jaguars beginning play as an expansion team. That meant 1994 would be a year to scout the league in hopes of finding hidden talent.

Mark was one of those hidden jewels.

"I wanted someone who could be the foundation for our team," said Coughlin. "I liked his athleticism, his courage, leadership and his ability to run. He was the quarterback we identified as the player we felt could best help us grow into a Super Bowl contender."

The Philadelphia Eagles felt the same way. Eagles coach Ray Rhodes, who had been the defensive coordinator of the Packers before being hired to coach the Eagles in 1995, used to watch Mark run the scout team against his defenses. He knew what he could do—which was move the ball—and he wanted him to do it for his Eagles.

The Eagles worked out a trade for Mark on one condition: They had to sign him to a new deal. The two sides negotiated for days, and the Eagles wanted Mark to sign a five-year contract. But they also said Randall Cunningham may be their starter for five years.

Mark was tired of sitting. The Eagles later lowered the deal to four years, but by then Mark was resigned to simply having a chance to play.

Jacksonville would be that chance.

With the deal to the Eagles falling apart, the Jaguars jumped into the talks. They offered Green Bay third- and fifth-round draft choices in the 1995 draft for Mark. The Packers agreed, and Mark agreed on a three-year contract, sealing the trade.

Two days before the first draft in Jaguars' history, the team acquired their franchise quarterback.

"The most important move this franchise ever made," said Coughlin.

Even more important for Mark.

"I knew it was an opportunity for me to play," Mark said. "I was ready. It was time for me to get that chance. When you're a rookie or in your second year, and you're in a place where you're not playing, you don't know what's going to happen. You've just got to take it year by year and hope for an opportunity. When one comes, you've got to take it."

Finally, after splitting time at Washington with Hobert, and then sitting behind Favre, Mark's time had come.

Now it was time to see what he would do with it.

Jacksonville's franchise quarterback. (Joe Robbins)

A Chance to Start

The depth chart told Jaguars fans all they needed to know about the team's quarterback situation that first year.

Steve Beuerlein, first. Mark was second.

Beuerlein was the first player the Jaguars selected in the expansion draft that year. He was a veteran who was left exposed by the Arizona Cardinals, a player who once helped lead the Dallas Cowboys to the playoffs when Troy Aikman was injured.

*A quarterback has to be quick on his feet to avoid the defense.
(Joe Robbins)*

Beuerlein was considered a smart quarterback with a so-so arm, but a guy who Coughlin thought would be perfect for a first-year team. Mark would wait his turn again.

The idea was for him to learn the offense, adjust to the idea of being a full-time starter, and then take over that role later in 1995 or perhaps in 1996.

In the third quarter of the team's first-ever game, that plan changed. Mark replaced Beuerlein that day in what turned into a 10-3 loss to the Houston Oilers. Neither played well, and the two shared time the next three games, with Mark getting his first NFL start against the New York Jets in the third week with Beuerlein injured.

It was anything but memorable.

"It sure wasn't pretty," Mark would say later.

Playing behind an offensive line that struggled, Mark ran for his life that day as the Jets beat the Jaguars, 27-10, at Giants Stadium. Mark was sacked

Mark points out the direction his team needs to go.
(Joe Robbins)

six times and his magical feet prevented another half dozen. He completed 15 of 33 passes for 138 yards, but much of that came long after the game was decided. At one point, Mark was six of 21. He did throw his first NFL touchdown pass, hitting Ernest Givens from seven yards out.

"Not quite a good first start, was it?" Mark said.

He again started the following week against the Packers, his former team, completing 16 of 29 for 156 yards and two touchdowns in a 24-14 loss. The Jaguars were then 0-4, and Mark was headed back on the bench.

Beuerlein was chosen to start against the Houston Oilers in the Astrodome on the first Sunday of October. But he struggled again, forcing Coughlin to once again turn to Mark.

This time, it was memorable.

Mark came off the bench in the fourth quarter to throw a 15-yard touchdown pass to Desmond

Howard with 1:09 left in the game to give the Jaguars their first-ever victory, 17-16.

"I just felt we needed to be picked up," said Coughlin. "That's why I went to Mark."

He hasn't left him since.

When healthy, Mark has started every game since that victory over the Oilers. He started eight more games that first season, missing three with a hamstring injury late in the season.

Mark finished the season completing 201 of 346 passes for 2,168 yards and 15 touchdowns. He closed out the season leaving little doubt as to who would be the team's starter in 1996.

On Christmas Eve, playing with a sore hamstring, he completed 17-of-29 passes for 275 yards and ran 27 yards for a touchdown to lead the Jaguars to a 24-21 victory over the Cleveland Browns. It was Mark who led the team on a five-play, 63-yard drive to the winning points in the final 1:13

of the game, the score coming on a 34-yard field goal by Mike Hollis with no time left.

"Write about No. 8 (Mark)," Coughlin said after the game. "He was 75-percent and he runs for a touchdown? It was a great effort, a gutsy effort on his part."

"I wish I was 75 percent," Mark said. "I was more around 60."

One thing was 100 percent: Mark was now officially an NFL starting quarterback.

"You saw how tough he was that day," said Jimmy Smith. "Our coaching staff saw we had a quarterback we can count on, a guy who can lead this team."

Mark was looking over his shoulder trying to spot an opponent who might try to bring him down. (Joe Robbins)

CHAPTER SIX

Full Time Starter

If it wasn't Mark's team by the first day of 1996, it was by that summer. That's when the Jaguars decided not to re-sign Beuerlein, who was an unrestricted free agent. Beuerlein would later sign with expansion rival, Carolina, leaving the Jaguars in the hands of Mark.

For the first time since high school, Mark didn't have to look over his shoulder. There was no Billy Joe Hobert. No Brett Favre. No Steve Beuerlein.

Mark barks out the cadence. (Joe Robbins)

The training-camp depth chart, for the first time in his NFL career, told the story he had waited so long to see. There on the line next to QB was Mark's name—first. Not second. Not listed as a backup.

Mark Brunell, full-time starter.

Finally.

"I'm comfortable with it," he said then.

He had little choice, but that's the way Mark wanted it. Remember the competitive desire that was spawned by his wrestling matches with his younger brother? That's what would drive him again.

"You want all the pressure on you," he said. "If you can't handle the pressure, you don't have any business being a starter in the NFL."

In 1996, Mark would prove he had every business being a starter, capping a dream season in the

Pro Bowl. It would be a season in which he took every snap of every game—the only quarterback in the league to do so—in leading the Jaguars to within one game of the Super Bowl.

Mark led the league in passing yards (4,367) and led all quarterbacks with 396 rushing yards. He became the first quarterback to lead in both categories since Johnny Unitas in 1963.

It wasn't a season without adversity, however.

The Jaguars may have made it to the AFC Championship Game, but at one point they were 4-7. Included in that slow start were some tough games for Mark. One loss to St. Louis was perhaps the low point in his career, even to this day, in terms of performance.

Mark completed 37 of 52 passes for 421 yards, but drive after drive came up empty inside the Red Zone. Mark was intercepted five times, all inside the Rams' 12 as the Jaguars lost, 17-14, to fall to 3-

5. After the game, Mark was visibly upset, getting testy with the media.

"I feel responsible for this one," Mark said. "A quarterback's job is not to throw interceptions."

Mark became the target of angry fans, many of whom supported Beuerlein in 1995. "Mark Brunell is putting up impressive numbers," one fan wrote. "But is he colorblind?"

The next night, while filming a TV show, Mark was the butt of a cruel joke. Someone from a local radio station presented Mark a box of five jelly-filled turnovers—one for each of Mark's interceptions.

Needless to say, times weren't good for Mark.

That's where the competitiveness came out again. Instead of folding, he responded to the critics, bouncing back with a huge season. Three weeks after the St. Louis debacle, he arrived as a team leader.

Mark looks on from the sideline.
(Joe Robbins)

Late in a 28-3 loss to the Pittsburgh Steelers at Three Rivers Stadium, Mark attempted to hit receiver Andre Rison on a seam route. But Rison, seeing a defender coming his way, pulled up, allowing Deon Figures to intercept the pass. Mark was infuriated, and as Rison walked off the field, Mark berated him, the first time he had done so publicly to a teammate. It was all caught by the NBC cameras.

After the game, Mark brushed aside the talk of a controversy. But it was evident that Rison was not one of his favorites, and the next day Rison was released. Rison had been a problem to the team since his signing in the summer, but clearly his release showed that Mark had arrived as a power player on the Jaguars.

Probably not coincidentally, the Jaguars didn't lose another game the rest of that season after Rison's release. They ripped off five consecutive victories to make the playoffs, then stunned the Buffalo Bills in the AFC wild-card game at Orchard Park, N.Y. The Jaguars' 30-27 victory was the first playoff loss at home for the Bills and Mark's first playoff victory as a starter.

Mark completed 18 of 33 for 239 yards and one touchdown, but he also threw two interceptions, one which was returned 38 yards for a touchdown by Jeff Burris.

"Who says we can't win when I throw interceptions?" Mark asked as he left the field that day, an obvious reference to the St. Louis game earlier in the season.

The next week he led the upset over the Broncos, transforming himself into an NFL star overnight. Denver was such a heavy favorite, few gave the Jaguars any chance of staying close, let alone winning.

When they fell behind 12-0, the game appeared on its way to being a blowout. But then the Jaguars came alive. Mark led them to scores on six consecutive possessions to engineer one of the biggest playoff upsets ever.

"We never faced a quarterback like that before," said Denver defensive end Alfred Williams after the game.

Sports Illustrated called him BrunElway after the game, having beaten Elway on his home field in Elway-like fashion—escaping rushers to make big plays in the passing game.

"That was special," Mark said.

The fairy-tale season came to an end for the Jaguars and Mark the following week. Playing in the frigid cold of Foxboro, Mass., the Jaguars lost 20-6 to the New England Patriots in the title game.

It was not a good day for Mark. One play in particular was especially haunting. With the Jag-

Mark was named MVP of the 1998 Pro Bowl.
(Joe Robbins)

uars trailing 13-6, Mark drove them to a first down at the New England six-yard line with just over four minutes in the game. But on the second play from the five, Mark's pass was intercepted in the end zone by Willie Clay.

"Just me not seeing the back-side safety," said Mark. "To have a scoring opportunity like that after a long drive and come away with nothing is going to bother me for a long time."

It didn't seem to bother him too long. Three weeks later, Mark was named the MVP of the Pro Bowl.

He was now an elite among the elite.

Mark's jersey, number 8, is a hot seller in Jacksonville.
(Joe Robbins)

Mark Mania

If 1996 was his coming-out year, 1997 would be even more special. Mark was now considered one of the top quarterbacks in the league. His face adorned preseason magazine covers and his No. 8 jersey was a hot seller in Jacksonville.

Mark Mania was alive.

Prior to the start of the 1997 training camp, Mark's agent was involved in serious contract talks to have his client paid like one of the best. Mark was entering the final year of his three-year contract with the Jaguars, meaning he could become an unrestricted free agent after the season.

The Jaguars weren't about to let him go anywhere.

To insure that, the team made him one of the highest-paid players in the league when Mark signed a new five-year, $31.5-million contract. If Mark wasn't yet a superstar, he was sure being paid like one.

"I'm just glad this was able to get done and I could concentrate on football," he said the day the contract was announced.

With that kind of money comes added pressure, something Mark was prepared to handle.

"The bar has gone up," he said that day. "I know that."

Mark loved the added pressure, almost relishing in it. He went out and had his best training camp with the Jaguars. His balls were on target, his touch better. The reads were improved as he tried to become more of a pocket passer and less of an athlete playing quarterback.

Safer that way, you know.

Or is it? In the middle of what was one of the high points in his life, Mark's good times came to a quick end. In the team's third preseason game against the New York Giants at Giants Stadium, the city of Jacksonville saw something that had only feared to that point:

Mark lying on the ground in agonizing pain, clutching his knee.

Giants linebacker Jesse Armstead had smashed into Mark's right knee in the second quarter of that game, causing the knee to bend back. As he hit the ground, Mark screamed out in pain.

The reactions of his teammates told the story that night. Most stood around him and prayed,

***Doctors feared Mark wouldn't be able to play after
a knee injury but their fears were laid to rest.
(Joe Robbins)***

shaking their heads from side to side, the grim reality being that they may be playing the season without their leader.

As a city of fans braced for news, Mark became the lead topic on daily newscasts.

"When Mark got hurt," said Jaguars owner Wayne Weaver, "people thought the world had come to an end. It was amazing how it dominated the news."

Doctors feared the worst, telling Mark he had a torn ACL, the same injury to the same leg he had suffered at Washington. But Mark thought differently. A strong religious faith kept him thinking the doctors were wrong.

Five days after the injury, Mark was right. As TV stations cut in for live updates, the Jaguars announced that Mark's ACL was only partially torn. He would play again that season.

"I told the media God had healed my knee," said Mark, a devoutly religious man. "My ACL was blown and then after the surgery, it wasn't blown. It was a miracle recovery."

Six weeks later, Mark would start against the Pittsburgh Steelers. When it became clear he would play that night, special T-shirts began making their way around Jacksonville.

On it was Mark's picture. The caption? Miracle Man.

Playing their first Monday night game ever, Mark led the Jaguars to a 30-21 victory over the rival Pittsburgh Steelers at Alltel Stadium. Mark completed 24-of-42 passes for 306 yards and one touchdown, showing few signs of the six weeks of inactivity.

"I had no problems whatsoever," Mark said. "Some of my throws weren't as accurate as they should have been. But it was good to get a game in."

The following week, the Jaguars lost for the first time in nine regular-season games, losing to the Washington Redskins. Mark struggled that day, completing 16-of-31 passes for 153 yards and two interceptions.

It was obvious that the adrenaline of the victory over the Steelers didn't carry over. Mark's mobility was clearly not the same as it had been prior to the injury, and the Redskins exposed that.

Now the city wasn't so sure their Miracle Man had made the right decision in his quick return from the injury. A poll in a local newspaper asked if he had come back too soon. The answer was an overwhelming yes.

"He's not going to scramble until we feel he's 100 percent," Coughlin said.

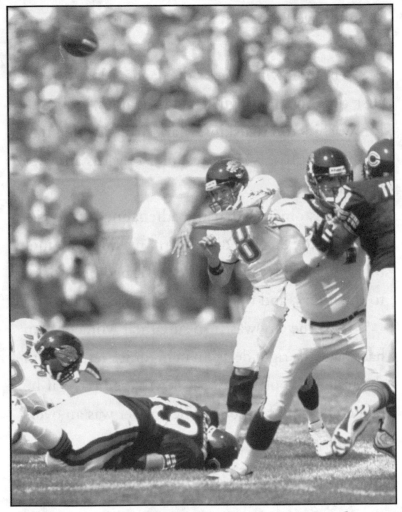

While injured, Mark learned to play better using the pocket pass. (Joe Robbins)

Mark would not be 100 percent the rest of the season. The once free-wheeling Mark, who would take off and turn a potential sack into a 27-yard gain, was not the same player. Mark would run just 48 times that season, down from the 80 the year before.

Despite the limited mobility, Mark was able to throw for 3,281 yards and 18 touchdown passes, earning his second straight trip to the Pro Bowl. He also cut his interceptions down to seven. He had grown as a quarterback, despite the injury.

"That brace really bothered me," he said. "I was never able to get comfortable."

Something good did come out of it, though. Forced to stay in the pocket, Mark became a better pocket passer. Where he once would take off at the first sign of pressure, he now stayed to wait for the second and third read.

"After running all over the place in college, people said I ran way too much," said Mark. "And that was the case. I ran too much and didn't tune my passing game. (In 1997), I was forced to sit in the pocket. Did it help me with my reads? Sure it did. But it didn't really make me a better quarterback. That's not what I do. That's not my style. I'm better when I can run around."

His play was good enough to lead the Jaguars into the playoffs for the second consecutive season. The team finished 11-5, second in the AFC Central to Pittsburgh.

That earned the Jaguars a return trip to Denver for an AFC wild-card game, where on the same field a year earlier, Mark had become a household name.

This time, it wasn't to be. The Broncos dominated the Jaguars from the start, eventually winning, 42-17. For Mark, it marked the end of an emotional roller-coaster season.

It started with the high of a new contract, and the certainty he wouldn't be leaving Jacksonville any time soon. Then there was the down of the knee injury, followed by the up of the Monday Night return, and then the down of the loss in Denver.

During that game, a botched center exchange between he and center Dave Widell ended a Jaguars' rally as they were driving, trailing 21-17. The Jaguars never recovered as Denver scored 21 unanswered points. Mark completed 18 of 32 passes for 203 yards, no touchdowns and one interception.

It was a far cry from his performance a year before.

Perhaps that's why the picture of Mark from that locker room following the game was one that had not been seen before. Amid the chaos of a post-

Mark tried hard to prove to fans he was the same quarterback even after his injury. (Joe Robbins)

game playoff frenzy, Mark was stoic and almost appeared to be in a sense of shock. The hurt was all over his face.

"I didn't play well," he said later. "I guess that's why I looked that way."

"He gets criticized for smiling after a loss, but inside it tears him up," said Boselli after that game. "That was hard for Mark. A lot of people kept telling him he wasn't the same quarterback. That can get to you."

Mark tries to scramble past oncoming opponents.
(Joe Robbins)

CHAPTER EIGHT

NFL Superstar

To help forget the sting of 1997, Mark traveled to St. Croix with Boselli and their wives for a week of relaxation. There, he felt, he could escape the trappings of being an NFL quarterback.

Surely, he would go unrecognized.

He didn't. A local recognized Mark, a tell-tale sign that he had arrived as an NFL superstar.

"You're Mark Brunell, the quarterback of the Jaguars," one of the workers in the hotel told him.

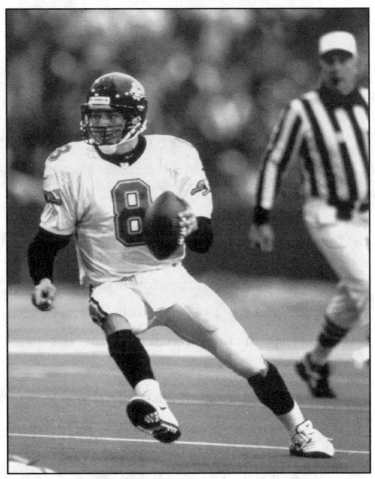

*Mark moving like his old self and leading his team.
(Joe Robbins)*

"Shh, don't tell anyone," Mark said.

"In the past, people always came up to me and asked me if I played football because I was so big," said Boselli. "They kind of figured it out. But they never really thought Mark played. This time, they knew him. Mark isn't in the background anymore. Mark is one of the best in the league, and someday he will lead this team to a Super Bowl."

As the 1998 season neared, Mark did put 1997 behind him. Forward, he thought, was the only way to go.

The Jaguars were being tabbed as a preseason favorite in the AFC to get to the Super Bowl. *Sports Illustrated* went so far as to pick them to win it, putting extra pressure on a team that had been dominated in its last game by the eventual Super Bowl-champion Broncos.

Most of the pressure was firmly on the shoulders of Mark. If the Jaguars were now his team, as many had suggested, then the pressure went with that claim.

"The quarterback can't be the reason we don't go to the Super Bowl," said Mark before the season. "In fact, the quarterback needs to be one of the reasons why we go to the Super Bowl, because he had his best year. There's no more of the, 'well, he's young. He's got to learn.' There's room for a lot of growth, but I need to go out there and have a big year for us. If I have a good year, the kind of year I think I should have, it will be a big year for us. That's all that matters. It's time for the young quarterback to have matured."

Mark was to make his 50th start of his career in 1998. That number of starts has had a direct correlation to success of recent NFL quarterbacks. Troy Aikman led the Dallas Cowboys to a Super Bowl victory in the season in which he started his

50th NFL game. New England's Bledsoe and Denver's Elway both took their teams to the Super Bowl in the season of their 50th start, only to lose the big game.

Favre and San Francisco's Young lost in the NFL Championship Game in their season of the 50th start.

"Interesting stat," Mark said before the 1998 season. "But no matter how many starts I've made, it's time for me to produce. It's time for me to get this team where it's supposed to go."

He took the team on his shoulders, and his teammates allowed that to happen.

"Oh, sure it's his team," said wide receiver Jimmy Smith. "It's always been his team. You can see the confidence growing in him. He's supposed to be good. What do you expect? It's his time. It will be a big deal if he isn't ready to take this team to the Super Bowl."

One of Mark's famous moments was an 87-yard drive that led to a victory over the Bears. (Joe Robbins)

"He may not show it, but it's definitely his team," said guard Ben Coleman. "Mark is the guy that drives this team, no question about it."

"It's his huddle," said wide receiver Keenan McCardell.

The Jaguars got off to a fast start in 1998, jumping to a 5-0 record and earning praise around the league. Maybe that Super Bowl talk was real. Mark, meanwhile, was also off to a good start.

He was back moving in and out of the pocket, running with the reckless abandon of 1996. His 12-play, 87-yard drive in the final minutes led to the winning touchdown in the opening victory against the Chicago Bears.

Afterward, Mark called it "the greatest drive in franchise history."

He continued to play well, having perhaps his best game ever in the third week, leading the Jaguars to a victory over Baltimore. Mark was 25 of 32

Despite injuries, Mark always comes back with a vengeance. (Joe Robbins)

for 376 yards, two touchdowns and no interceptions.

"Mark Brunell is one of the best quarterbacks in the league," Jimmy Smith said after that game. "We're just fortunate as receivers to have a quarterback like Mark."

After winning their first five, the team lost two in a row, losing again to those hated Broncos. But the Jaguars regrouped behind Mark to win four of their next five. The playoffs were a certainty, and a first-round bye was possible.

Then it happened again, the nightmarish vision for Jaguars fans of seeing Mark down on the ground in agonizing pain, clutching his left ankle. Mark had suffered a severely sprained left ankle in the 13th game against the Detroit Lions, an injury that forced him to the sidelines.

"I've never had a sprained ankle before—ever," said Mark after the game. "So I don't know what to

Mark's teammates rely on his presence as much as his ability. (Brian Spurlock)

think. It's so frustrating to get hurt at this time of the year. I don't know what to think. Hopefully, it's not too bad."

That wasn't to be the case. Mark would miss the final three games of the season as the Jaguars lost two of their final three to finish 11-5. It was clear this team had no chance in the playoffs without him.

"Will he play?" became the most-asked question in Jacksonville.

Mark was able to play in the AFC wild-card game against the Patriots, the first-ever playoff game at Jacksonville's Alltel Stadium. Limping noticeably, Mark was able to complete 14 of 31 passes for 161 yards and a touchdown.

More than his numbers, his presence was key that day.

"Just seeing No. 8 trotting into the huddle gives this offense confidence," McCardell said that day.

Mark is known as a tough guy and a hard worker. (Joe Robbins)

"It makes you think everything is going to be all right."

A week later the Jaguars lost to the New York Jets in the AFC Divisional playoffs, ending their chance to get to the Super Bowl. Mark again showed the signs of the ankle injury, struggling at times to make the throws. Later he would admit that he was 70-percent that day, a percentage that would send most to the sidelines.

"He's a tough guy, no doubt about it," said Coughlin.

A tough guy who has become one of the best quarterbacks in the league, one who drives the Jaguars. They are his team, and it will be his play that could sometime in the near future get this team to the Super Bowl.

Mark was right all along: Football over baseball was the right choice.

There's no debating that now.

Mark Brunell Quick Facts

Name: Mark Brunell

Team: Jacksonville Jaguars

Position: Quarterback

Number: 8

Height/Weight: 6-1, 218 lbs.

Birthdate: September 17, 1970

Hometown: Los Angeles, California

Years in the League: 7

How acquired: Trade from Green Bay 1995

Drafted: Fifth Round (118 overall)

College: University of Washington

1998 Highlight: Led the Jaguars to an 11-5 record and First Place in the AFC Central.

Statistical Highlight: Led the AFC in passing in 1997 with a career-best 91.2 rating

Little known for: As a senior in high school, Mark was named to The Sporting News top 100 for football.

Mark Brunell Career Statistics

Regular Season: *Passing*

Year	Team	GP	ATT	CMP	PCT	YDS	TD	INT
1993	Green Bay	0	0	0	.000	0	0	0
1994	Green Bay	2	27	12	.444	95	0	0
1995	Jacksonville	13	346	201	.581	2,168	15	7
1996	Jacksonville	16	557	353	.634	4,367	19	20
1997	Jacksonville	14	435	264	.607	3,281	18	7
1998	Jacksonville	16	354	208	.588	2,601	20	9
TOTALS		**61**	**1,719**	**1,038**	**.604**	**12,512**	**72**	**43**

Regular Season: *Rushing*

Year	Team	ATT	YDS	AVG	LG	TD
1993	Green Bay	0	0	0.0	0	0
1994	Green Bay	6	7	1.2	5	1
1995	Jacksonville	67	480	7.2	27	4
1996	Jacksonville	80	396	5.0	33	3
1997	Jacksonville	48	257	5.4	15	2
1998	Jacksonville	49	192	3.9	18	0
TOTALS		**250**	**1,332**	**5.3**	**33**	**10**

Jacksonville Jaguars Passing Records

Career

Passing Yards	Mark Brunell, 1995-98	12,417
Passing TD	Mark Brunell, 1995-98	72

Single Season

Passing Yards	Mark Brunell, 1996	4,367
Passing TD	Mark Brunell, 1998	20

Single Game

Passing Yards	Mark Brunell, 9/22/96	432
Passing TD	Mark Brunell, 11/29/98	5

Prolific Passer

In 1996, Mark Brunell had the fifth-most prolific single-season total yardage by a quarterback in NFL history. He passed for 4,367 yards and rushing for 396 yards, accounting for combined yardage of 4,763.

Player, Team	Year	Total	Pass	Rush
1. Dan Marino, Miami	1984	5,077	5,084	-7
2. Warren Moon, Houston	1990	4,904	4,689	215
3. Dan Fouts, San Diego	1981	4,858	4,802	56
4. Neil Lomax, St. Louis	1984	4,798	4,614	184
5. Mark Brunell, Jacksonville	**1996**	**4,763**	**4,367**	**396**
6. Warren Moon, Houston	1991	4,758	4,690	68

Mark Brunell's 1998 Passing Statistics

PASSING

Date	Opp	Comp	Att	Yds	Pct	TD	Int
09/06/98	@Chi	22	35	207	.629	2	2
09/13/98	KC	11	18	126	.611	1	0
09/20/98	Bal	25	34	376	.735	2	0
09/27/98	@Ten	17	28	155	.607	2	2
10/12/98	Mia	12	18	213	.667	2	1
10/18/98	@Buf	16	28	19	.571	0	0
10/25/98	@Den	28	46	353	.609	3	0
11/01/98	@Bal	13	20	237	.650	2	1
11/08/98	Cin	5	12	111	.417	1	0
11/15/98	TB	22	37	248	.595	0	0
11/22/98	@Pit	18	42	212	.429	1	3
11/29/98	@Cin	19	35	244	.543	4	0
12/06/98	Det	0	1	0	0	0	0
TOTALS		**208**	**354**	**2,061**	**.581**	**20**	**9**

1998 NFL Leaders: Passing Yardage

1.	Brett Favre	Green Bay Packers	4,212
2.	Steve Young	San Francisco 49ers	4,170
3.	Peyton Manning	Indianapolis Colts	3,739
4.	Jake Plummer	Arizona Cardinals	3,737
5.	Randall Cunningham	Minnesota Vikings	3,704
6.	Drew Bledsoe	New England Patriots	3,633
7.	Dan Marino	Miami Dolphins	3,497
8.	Trent Green	Washington Redskins	3,441
9.	Vinny Testaverde	New York Jets	3,256
10.	Steve McNair	Tennessee Oilers	3,228
11.	Chris Chandler	Atlanta Falcons	3,154
12.	John Elway	Denver Broncos	2,806
13.	Trent Dilfer	Tampa Bay Buccaneers	2,729
14.	Doug Flutie	Buffalo Bills	2,711
15.	Steve Beuerlein	Carolina Panthers	2,613
16.	**Mark Brunell**	**Jacksonville Jaguars**	**2,601**
17.	Kordell Stewart	Pittsburgh Steelers	2,560
18.	Tony Banks	St. Louis Rams	2,535
19.	Troy Aikman	Dallas Cowboys	2,330
20.	Rich Gannon	Kansas City Chiefs	2,305

Mark Brunell's Jaguar Highlights

1998

• Jacksonville won the AFC Central Division championship with an 11-5 record, beating New England (25-10) in the wild-card playoff, then losing to the New York Jets (34-24) in the divisional playoffs.

• Statistically, Mark finished fourth among AFC passers with a rating of 89.9, and seventh among all NFL quarterbacks.

• Mark's 2,601 yards was the third-best single-season total in Jaguars' history.

1997

• The Jaguars compiled an 11-5 regular-season record, finishing second in the AFC Central, losing at Denver (42-19) in the wild-card playoff game.

• Mark led the AFC and ranked third in the NFL with a career-high 91.2 passer rating.

• Despite missing two games, Mark ranked ninth in the NFL in passing yards, third in average gain per pass, fourth in completion percentage and 13th in touchdowns.

• Mark played in his second Pro Bowl, starting at quarterback for the AFC squad.

1996

• Despite compiling just a 9-7 record during the regular season, good for second place in the AFC Central, Jacksonville caught fire in the playoffs. The Jaguars beat Buffalo (30-27) in the wild-card playoff, Denver (30-27) in the division playoff, then lost at New England (20-6) in the AFC championship game.

• Mark led all NFL quarterbacks in passing yards (4,367) and led all QBs in rushing yards (396), becoming the first signal-caller since Baltimore's Johnny Unitas in 1963 to lead the NFL in both categories.

• He moved into 13th place on the single-season passing yardage list, averaging 273 yards per game.

• Mark was the only quarterback in the NFL to take every snap for his team.

• He led the NFL with six 300-yard passing games and two 400-yard passing contests.

• Mark earned his first trip to the Pro Bowl and was named Player of the Game after leading the AFC to a 26-23 overtime victory over the NFC.

1995

• Jacksonville compiled a 4-12 record, fifth-best in the AFC Central.

• Mark led the Jaguars to all four of their victories in their inaugural season. Two of the victories came against Cleveland, one was at Houston, and the fourth was at home versus Pittsburgh.

• He became the highest-rated passer ever for an NFL expansion team.

• Mark took over as starter at quarterback for the last 11 weeks of the season, finishing with an 82.6 passer rating to rank seventh in the AFC and 15th in the NFL.

• He rushed for 480 yards, the AFC's first quarterback to rush for 400 or more yards since 1983.

Baseball Superstar Series Titles
Collect Them All!

___ Mark McGwire: Mac Attack!

___ #1 *Derek Jeter: The Yankee Kid*

___ #2 *Ken Griffey Jr.: The Home Run Kid*

___ #3 *Randy Johnson: Arizona Heat!*

___ #4 *Sammy Sosa: Slammin' Sammy*

___ #5 *Bernie Williams: Quiet Superstar*

___ #6 *Omar Vizquel: The Man with the Golden Glove*

___ #7 *Mo Vaughn: Angel on a Mission*

___ #8 *Pedro Martinez: Throwing Strikes*

___ #9 *Juan Gonzalez: Juan Gone!*

___ #10 *Tony Gwynn: Mr. Padre*

___ #11 *Kevin Brown: Kevin with a "K"*

___ #12 *Mike Piazza: Mike and the Mets*

___ #13 *Larry Walker: Canadian Rocky*

___ #14 *Nomar Garciaparra: High 5!*

___ #15 *Sandy and Roberto Alomar: Baseball Brothers*

___ #16 *Mark Grace: Winning with Grace*

___ #17 *Curt Schilling: Phillie Phire!*

___ #18 *Alex Rodriguez: A+ Shortstop*

___ #19 *Roger Clemens: Rocket!*

Only $4.95 per book!

Football Superstar Series Titles
Collect Them All!

___ #1 *Ed McCaffrey: Catching a Star*

___ #3 *Peyton Manning: Passing Legacy*

___ #4 *Jake Plummer: Comeback Cardinal*

___ #5 *Mark Brunell: Super Southpaw*

___ #6 *Drew Bledsoe: Patriot Rifle*

___ #7 *Junior Seau: Overcoming the Odds*

___ #8 *Marshall Faulk: Rushing to Glory*

Only $4.95 per book!

Basketball Superstar Series Titles
Collect Them All!

_____ #1 *Kobe Bryant: The Hollywood Kid*

_____ #2 *Keith Van Horn: Nothing But Net*

_____ #3 *Antoine Walker: Kentucky Celtic*

_____ #4 *Kevin Garnett: Scratching the Surface*

_____ #5 *Tim Duncan: Slam Duncan*

_____ #6 *Reggie Miller: From Downtown*

_____ #7 *Jason Kidd: Rising Sun*

_____ #8 *Vince Carter: Air Canada*

Only $4.95 per book!

Call Toll Free: 1-877-424-BOOK (2665) or visit us at www.sportspublishinginc.com

Hockey Superstar Series Titles
Collect Them All!

____ #1 *John LeClair: Flying High*

____ #2 *Mike Richter: Gotham Goalie*

____ #3 *Paul Kariya: Maine Man*

____ #4 *Dominik Hasek: The Dominator*

____ #5 *Jaromir Jagr: Czechmate*

____ #6 *Martin Brodeur: Picture Perfect*

____ #8 *Ray Bourque: Bruins Legend*

Only $4.95 per book!